**Age of dinosaurs. Dinosaurs are at their peak in size, variety and numbers and dominate every continent.**

**'K-T extinction'. End of the dinosaurs.**

Mesozoic era

248 MYA – 65 MYA

Cretaceous period

144 MYA – 65 MYA

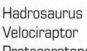

Hadrosaurus
Velociraptor
Protoceratops

Centrosaurus
Troodon
Tyrannosaurus
Triceratops
Ankylosaurus
Edmontosaurus

Giganotosaurus
Spinosaurus

Argentinosaurus
Nodosaurus

Deinonychus

Acrocanthosaurus

Iguanadon

Baryonyx

3

# FULL TIMELINE

Oceans and atmosphere form. Earliest life forms in oceans.

Trilobites dominate seas. Still no land life.

Earliest land plants appear.

Insects flourish. First reptiles evolve. Shrubs, ferns and trees dominate land.

Massive volcanic eruptions cause mass extinctions, wiping out 90% of marine life and 70% of land life!

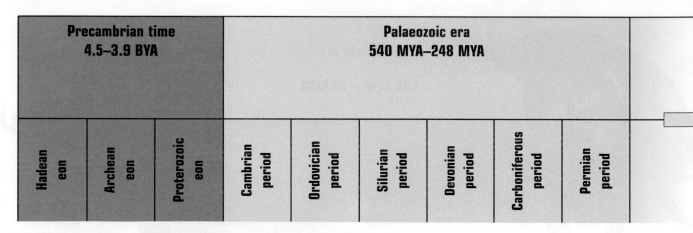

| Precambrian time 4.5–3.9 BYA | | | Palaeozoic era 540 MYA–248 MYA | | | | | | |
|---|---|---|---|---|---|---|---|---|---|
| Hadean eon | Archean eon | Proterozoic eon | Cambrian period | Ordovician period | Silurian period | Devonian period | Carboniferous period | Permian period | |

The Earth forms!

Sea plants begin photosynthesis.

First fish evolve.

Fish dominate oceans. Spiders and mites are first land creatures. First amphibians evolve. First forests form.

Synapsids, such as Dimetrodon and amphibians such as Eryops dominate land.

'K-T extinction'
End of the
dinosaurs.

Dinosaurs
dominate.
First mammals
evolve.

Mammals such
as horses, bats
and whales
evolve.

Most modern
birds and
mammals have
evolved.

'Great Ice Age'
Neanderthals and
Homo sapiens, or modern
humans, evolve.
Smilodon (sabre-toothed
tiger), mastodons and
mammoths evolve.

| Mesozoic era 248 MYA–65 MYA | | | Cenozoic era 65 MYA–NOW | | | | | | | |
|---|---|---|---|---|---|---|---|---|---|---|
| | | | Tertiary period (65 MYA – 1.8MYA) | | | | | | Quaternary period (1.8MYA – NOW) | |
| Triassic period | Jurassic period | Cretaceous period | Paleocene epoch | Eocene epoch | Oligocene epoch | Miocene epoch | Pliocene epoch | | Pleistocene epoch | Holocene epoch |

Sauropsids
such as the
archosaurs
dominate.
First cynodonts
such as
Cynognathus
evolve.
Marine reptiles
evolve.

**Age of
dinosaurs.
Dinosaurs are
at their peak in
size, variety and
numbers and
dominate every
continent.**

Mammals
dominate.
Early carnivores
evolve.

Creodonts
evolve.
Modern
mammals
become
dominant.

Hominids, the
ape-like
ancestors of
humans evolve.
Thylacosmilus
and other early
sabre-tooths
evolve.

Last ice
age ends.
Human
civilisation
develops.

# TYRANNOSAURUS REX

## King of the tyrant lizards

### FOSSIL FACTS
**Fossils have been found in several places in the USA and also in Mongolia.**

Powerful hind legs and very large feet would have enabled Tyrannosaurus Rex to walk and, probably even run for long distances in search of food. Even though its hands were tiny, they were armed with savage claws for ripping and tearing flesh from its prey. Its sharp teeth allowed it to rip flesh from a carcass and it could crush and grind the bones with its powerful jaw. It was also an opportunistic feeder and would also scavenge for dead animals whenever fresh food was in short supply.

Tyrannosaurus Rex was one of the biggest and most powerful dinosaurs. It was first discovered in 1902 and was named in 1905.

Tyrannosaurus Rex probably lived in family groups. Smaller dinosaurs would have been subjected its fierce and often fatal attacks. Large Tyrannosaurus Rex bite marks have been identified in the fossils of other dinosaurs.

## Dinosaur Data

| | |
|---|---|
| PRONUNCIATION: | TIE-RAN-O-SAW-RUS REX |
| SUBORDER: | THERAPODA |
| FAMILY: | TYRANNOSAUROIDEA |
| DESCRIPTION: | LARGE, POWERFUL CARNIVORE |
| FEATURES: | DOMINANT PREDATOR |
| DIET: | HUNTED AND SCAVENGED |

| Permian period | Triassic period | Jurassic period | Cretaceous period |
|---|---|---|---|
| 290-248 million years ago) | (248-176 million years ago) | (176-130 million years ago) | (130-66 million years ago) |

## Appearance

Tyrannosaurus Rex was 4.5–6 m (15–20 ft) tall and would have been able to see through the tops of the trees in the swampy forest it lived in.

The most recently discovered Tyrannosaurus Rex fossil was found in South Dakota in 1990; she's been called Sue after the woman who found her and is now on display in the Field Museum in Chicago.

# MEGA FACTS

- Over 12 m (39 ft) long from the nose to the end of tail.

- Could move at 16–48 km/h (10–30 mph).

- Powerful jaw of 58 serrated teeth each 15 cm (6 in.) long which re-grew when they were damaged.

- 200 bones in a full Tyrannosaurus skeleton – roughly the same number as a human.

- Fossil Sue was auctioned at Sotheby's for $7.6 million in 1997.

Dinosaur experts continue to search for new fossils and examine those already found to learn more about how this giant carnivore lived and died.

# GIGANOTOSAURUS

## Giant southern lizard (new king of the carnivores)

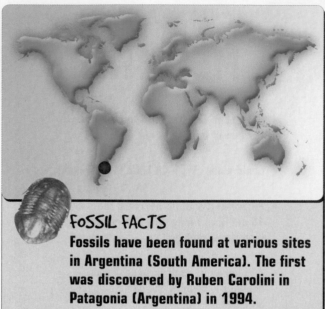

### FOSSIL FACTS
**Fossils have been found at various sites in Argentina (South America). The first was discovered by Ruben Carolini in Patagonia (Argentina) in 1994.**

Giganotosaurus means 'Giant Southern Lizard'. It was given its name in 1995 by Coria and Salgado.

Giganotosaurus lived at the same time as enormous plant-eating dinosaurs like Argentinosaurus which it could hunt and eat. Like Tyrannosaurus Rex, which lived 30 million years later, it hunted in warm, swampy areas.

## Appearance

Giganotosaurus was 5.5 m (18 ft) high and measured up to 15 m (49 ft) long but is not the largest dinosaur of all time; Argentinosaurus is the largest dinosaur at the moment and there may be more that we have not discovered yet. In 2006, scientists suggested that Gigantosaurus now been displaced as largest carnivore by Spinosaurus, based on a study of new finds.

Although larger than T-Rex, Giganotosaurus was more lightly built, and it is thought it could run quite fast. Its slender, pointed tail would have helped to balance it out as it ran, probably moving from side to side. It would also have helped Giganotosaurus make quick turns. From its skull, we know that it probably had a good sense of smell and excellent eyesight thanks to its large eyes.

Giganotosaurus walked on two legs, had a long slim tail, and had enormous jaws in its 1.8 m (6 ft) skull.

## Attacking prey

Those jaws were lined with serrated teeth, well adapted for slicing into flesh and up to 20 cm (8 in.) long.

| Permian period | Triassic period | Jurassic period | |
|---|---|---|---|
| 290-248 million years ago) | (248-176 million years ago) | (176-130 million years ago) | |

It did not have the powerful crushing bite of T-Rex, and so would have attacked by slashing. It had three clawed fingers it could use to slash, or grasp with.

When hunting, it would probably have singled out dinosaurs that were young, or weak, or separated from the herd. Fossil evidence where several skeletons were found close together suggests that they may have hunted and lived in packs.

Giganotosaurs may have cooperated in tasks like hunting and protecting their young.

# MEGA FACTS

- Weighed as much as 125 people.

- Appeared in 3-D in the IMAX® film *Dinosaurs*. Also in the *Walking with dinosaurs* special *Land of giants*, in which a pack of Giganotosaurs bring down an Argentinosaurus.

- The biggest Giganotosaurus was over a metre longer and a ton heavier than 'Sue', the largest known Tyrannosaurus Rex.

- May have hunted prey up to ten times its own size.

- Giganotosaurus had a skull the size of a bathtub, but its brain was only the size (and shape) of a banana.

**Note** This is not the same dinosaur as the African sauropod Gigantosaurus (different spelling) named by Seeley in 1869.

## Dinosaur Data

| | |
|---|---|
| PRONUNCIATION: | JIG-A-**NOT**-OH-**SAWR**-US |
| SUBORDER: | THERAPODA |
| FAMILY: | ALLOSAURIDAE |
| DESCRIPTION: | LARGE POWERFUL CARNIVORE |
| FEATURES: | DOMINANT PREDATOR |

# DEINONYCHUS

## Cunning bipedal hunter

### FOSSIL FACTS
The first fossils were found in 1964 by Grant E. Meyer and John H. Ostrom in southern Montana.

The name Deinonychus means 'terrible claw' and comes from the Greek words *deinos* (terrible) and *onychus* (claw). The name was given by John Ostrom in 1969 because of the long, wickedly sharp claw found on the second toe of each of its feet.

## Appearance

This carnivorous dinosaur was bipedal. It was about 1.5 m (4 ft) tall, weighed about 80 kg (176 lb) and measured 3 m (10 ft) from the tip of its nose to the end of its long, rigid tail. It had a large head with powerful jaws and sharp serrated teeth. Large eye sockets indicate it probably also had excellent eyesight.

| Permian period | Triassic period | Jurassic period | Cretaceous period |
|---|---|---|---|
| 290-248 million years ago) | (248-176 million years ago) | (176-130 million years ago) | (130-66 million years ago) |

Its feet were four-toed and it was the second toe that sported the vicious 13 cm (5 in.) long claw after which it was named. This claw could be held up out of the way whilst the creature was running, only snapping into position when needed for the attack. Deinonychus also had a pair of arms that ended in three-fingered hands with each finger having a curved claw that was long and sharp.

## The long claw

Initially, it was thought that the long claw on its second toe was used to slash prey but recent tests have shown that it was actually more likely used as a stabbing weapon. Deinonychus' likely method of attack was to use its powerful back legs to leap into the air and land on its prey, kicking the long sickle toe-claws in, causing significant damage and anchoring it firmly. It would then tear and bite at the prey to cause as much blood loss as possible.

Its long tail was stiffened with bony rods along the spine. This tail would have acted like a counterweight, giving Deinonychus excellent balance and allowing it to make very fast turns as it chased down prey. We also strongly believe that Deinonychus hunted in packs, as several fossils of groups of Deinonychus have been found. Hunting in packs would have allowed Deinonychus to take on prey that would be too large for a single Deinonychus.

## Brain size

The dromaeosauridae family all have quite large brains in comparison to their total body size, indicating that they were probably much more intelligent than other dinosaurs. This would have allowed them to work together as a team during the hunt and use simple tactics to guide their prey towards other members of the pack.

# MEGA FACTS

- Fossil evidence shows Deinonychus packs hunted and killed Tenontosaurus, a dinosaur ten times their size.

- There is some evidence that Deinonychus may have had feathers.

*Deinonychus*

## Dinosaur Data

| | |
|---|---|
| PRONUNCIATION: | DYN-**ON**-IK-US |
| SUBORDER: | THEROPODA |
| FAMILY: | DROMAEOSAURIDAE |
| DESCRIPTION: | FAST, AGILE BIPEDAL PREDATOR |
| FEATURES: | SICKLE CLAW ON EACH FOOT, LARGE BRAINS, LONG RIGID TAIL |
| DIET: | CARNIVOROUS |

# COMPSOGNATHUS

## Tiny, fleet-footed predator

### FOSSIL FACTS
**Fossils have been found in France and Germany, and possibly Portugal. The first specimen was discovered in Bavaria, Germany, in the late 1850s by Dr Oberndorfer.**

that Compsognathus was capable of rapid acceleration, high speed, flexibility, and quick reactions.

We know its size from two almost complete skeletons. Study of other partial skeletons gives a range of size from 70–140 cm (28–56 in.). It weighed only around 3.6 kg (8 lb) when fully-grown, and stood not much more than half a metre (1ft 6 in.) tall.

Palaeontologists cannot agree over whether Compsognathus had two or three fingers on each hand. Either way, those slender fingers would have helped

Compsognathus means 'elegant jaw' and comes from the Greek words *kompos* (elegant) and *gnathos* (jaw). It was named for the delicate bones of its lightly-built skull. It was given this name in 1859, by Johann A. Wagner.

Compsognathus was an early member of a group of dinosaurs called the coelurosaurs ('hollow-tail lizards'). Later members of the coelurosaur group included the most likely ancestors of birds. Compsognathus had hollow bones throughout its body. This made it very light and fast.

### Appearance

Compsognathus ran on its long, thin hind legs and had surprisingly short arms. It had a long tail to act as a counterbalance and to stabilise it during fast turns. Its head was small and pointed and it had a long, flexible neck. Its skull suggests it had good eyesight and was probably pretty intelligent. The characteristics of its skull and legs tell us

| Permian period | Triassic period | Jurassic period | Cretaceous period |
|---|---|---|---|
| 290-248 million years ago) | (248-176 million years ago) | (176-130 million years ago) | |

with grasping prey, which could then be swallowed whole or torn into pieces by tiny, sharp teeth.

## Habitat

At the time Compsognathus lived, water covered much of what is now France and southern Germany. Compsognathus lived on islands in this sea. Although very small, it was probably the largest predator where it lived – the small islands did not have enough vegetation to support large herbivores, which in turn meant there was no tempting prey for large carnivores.

# MEGA FACTS

- Compsognathus appeared in *Jurassic Park II* and *Jurassic Park III* as the vicious 'compys'. These films showed them hunting in packs, but in fact we have no idea whether they did this or not.

- Even fully grown, Compsognathus would weigh no more than a turkey.

- According to calculations made using the distance between fossilised footprints, Compsognathus could run at speeds up to 40 km/h (25 mph).

- The first fossil skeleton of this dinosaur that was found had the remains of a fast-running lizard called bavarisaurus in its stomach.

- In recent years the remains of even smaller dinosaurs have been found. These included the 50 cm (18 in.) long plant-eating Micropachycephalosaurus, which as well as being the smallest dinosaur in the world also has the longest name!

- Evidence of feathers has yet to be discovered on a Compsognathus fossil.

## Dinosaur Data

| | |
|---|---|
| PRONUNCIATION: | KOMP-SOG-**NAY**-THUS OR KOMP-SO-**NATH**-US |
| SUBORDER: | THEROPODA |
| FAMILY: | COMPSOGNATHIDAE |
| DESCRIPTION: | BIPEDAL CARNIVORE |
| FEATURES: | HOLLOW BONES |
| DIET: | SMALL ANIMALS |

# DROMAEOSAURUS

## Swift and deadly bipedal hunter

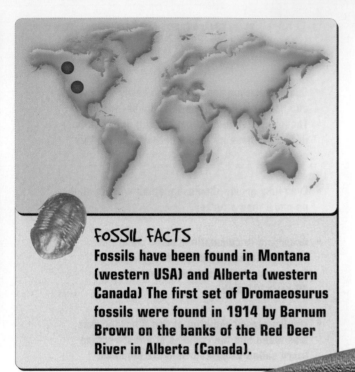

**Fossils have been found in Montana (western USA) and Alberta (western Canada) The first set of Dromaeosurus fossils were found in 1914 by Barnum Brown on the banks of the Red Deer River in Alberta (Canada).**

It had a large head, containing a big brain — scientists believe it was one of the most intelligent of the dinosaurs. It also had excellent vision thanks to its large eyes, and probably a strong sense of smell and good hearing, making it an efficient hunter. Its jaws were long and strong, and contained long, razor-sharp teeth.

## Attack

Dromaeosaurus' most dangerous weapons were its claws, which were sickle-shaped and on the end of each finger. Prey was probably gripped with the claws of the foot, while the

Dromaeosaurus means 'fast-running lizard'. It was given this name in 1922 by Barnum Brown and William Matthew. It is part of a group of dinosaurs known as dromaeosaurs, which are the dinosaurs believed to be most closely related to modern day birds.

When first discovered, Dromaeosaurus was hard to classify. It wasn't until nearly 50 years after its discovery that Dromaeosaurus was formally classified into its own family.

## Appearance

Dromaeosaurus was active and agile. It was about the size of a large dog, and balanced itself while running (and even standing on one leg so as to slash at prey with its clawed toes) with the help of its long, stiff tail.

The tail was stiffened by a lattice of bony rods and was flexible at the base so that it could be moved up and down

*Fossil of a juvenile Sinonithosaurus*

*Skeleton of a Dromaeosaurus*

# MEGA FACTS

- Dromaeosaurus teeth have been found among the fossils of much larger dinosaurs, leading some scientists to suggest that they hunted in packs like wolves, so that they could bring down larger prey.

- With its deep, large jaw, short and massive skull, and big strong teeth, Dromaeosaurus closely resembles the much larger Tyrannosaurs.

- In 2001, a remarkable fossilised skeleton was loaned from China to the American Museum of Natural History. Scientists believe it to be that of a Dromaeosaurus – with feathers from head to foot!

- It ate small and medium-sized plant eaters like young Triceratops and baby duckbills.

- All 'raptors' (as dromaeosaurs came to be nicknamed) have the sickle-shaped killing claw on the hind feet – this was used for disembowelling prey.

finger claws slashed at the victim, though the sharp, hooked claw on each leg could certainly do some horrendous damage of its own. Dromaeosaurus probably hunted by running and leaping at its prey, enabling it to use all four limbs in the attack as it launched itself at the target.

## Dinosaur Data

| | |
|---|---|
| PRONUNCIATION: | **DROH**-MEE-OH-**SAWR**-US |
| SUBORDER: | THEROPODA |
| FAMILY: | DROMAEOSAURIDAE |
| DESCRIPTION: | ACTIVE, AGILE BIPEDAL HUNTER |
| FEATURES: | MASSIVE SLASHING CLAWS |
| DIET: | CARNIVORE, POSSIBLE SCAVENGER |

15

# VELOCIRAPTOR

## Swift and vicious bipedal carnivore

### FOSSIL FACTS
**Fossils have been found in China, Mongolia and Russia. The first Velociraptor fossils were found in 1914.**

around 80 sharp bladed teeth – some of the teeth were over 2.5 cm (1 in.) long. It possessed large eyes, which gave it excellent vision even in the dark.

Velociraptor had an enlarged second toe with a vicious oversized claw attached to it. These sickle-like claws could be raised off the ground while running or walking, then used once the Velociraptor launched an attack.

Velociraptor means 'speedy thief'. This carnivore lived in a desert-like environment around 70 million years ago, and may have hunted in packs, preying largely on herbivores like Hadrosaurus.

### Appearance

It was about 1.5–2 m (5–6 ft), and stood on two legs. It had long arms and a long straight tail. Its strong jaws contained

### Dinosaur Data

| | |
|---|---|
| PRONUNCIATION: | VUH-**LOSS**-IH-**RAP**-TOR |
| SUBORDER: | THERAPODA |
| FAMILY: | DROMAESORIDAE |
| DESCRIPTION: | SMALL, SWIFT CARNIVORE |
| FEATURES: | VERY INTELLIGENT, BIPEDAL |
| DIET: | HUNTED AND POSSIBLY SCAVENGED |

| Permian period | Triassic period | Jurassic period | Cretaceous period |
|---|---|---|---|
| (290-248 million years ago) | (248-176 million years ago) | (176-130 million years ago) | (130-66 million years ago) |

## The claw experiments

In 2005 Dr Phil Manning performed experiments using a robotic claw designed to mimic the attack of a Velociraptor. The results showed that, against larger prey with tough skin, the claw would not have made wounds deep enough to kill quickly. The large claws were probably used to pierce and hold prey. Its razor-sharp teeth would then tear into the prey, causing as much blood loss as possible to vulnerable areas.

# MEGA FACTS

- Recent scientific thinking is that Velociraptor was very close to being birdlike, and may well have been covered in primitive feathers for warmth and display.

- Scientists believe a Velociraptor could leap up to 3.6 m (12 ft) to attack its prey.

- Velociraptor could run up to about 60 km/h (37 mph).

- They were probably warm-blooded in some degree.

- The Velociraptor had a very big brain compared to its body size, making it one of the most intelligent of the dinosaurs.

## Breathing

Some scientists now believe raptors could have had a way of breathing like modern birds. Birds store extra air in air sacs inside their hollow bones as well as using their lungs – this means they can extract oxygen from air much more efficiently than mammals. A comparison between bird anatomy and fossilised dinosaur remains revealed many similarities.

## Fossilised attack

An especially interesting fossil was discovered in 1971 in the Gobi Desert – it revealed a Velociraptor in mid-attack on a Protoceratops. The claws of the Velociraptor were buried in the body of the Protoceratops, its sickle claws close to where the jugular vein would have been – but the Protoceratops has the raptor's arm firmly in its jaws. Both seem to have died in a sudden sandstorm, or landslip, preserving their battle forever.

# OVIRAPTOR PHILOCARATOPS

## Odd-looking omnivorous raptor

### FOSSIL FACTS
**Fossils have been found in Mongolia. The first fossils were found in the Gobi Desert in 1924.**

Oviraptor philoceratops means 'egg thief, fond of horned dinosaurs'.

Oviraptor was a small, fast-moving biped with long slender legs and short arms for grasping. At the ends of these arms were large three-fingered hands with claws up to 8 cm (3 in.) long. It had a flexible neck, a long tail, its powerful jaws were designed for crushing and its skull was almost parrot-shaped. On top of its snout was a thin bony crest, which seemed to change with age.

The shape of Oviraptor's head and mouth would have made it equipped for dealing with a variety of food. It was probably an omnivore, making up its diet from almost anything it could find – for example, meat, plants, eggs, insects and shellfish. Omnivorous dinosaurs are very rare.

*Fossil*

# MEGA FACTS

- Oviraptor could run at about 70 km/h (43 mph).

- It was 1.8–2.5 m (6–8 ft) long and weighed about 36 kg (80 lb).

- If an Oviraptor sat on its eggs to keep them warm, that would mean it was warm-blooded. However, they may have sat on their eggs for other reasons, like protecting them.

- Its crest may have been used for mating display, or to distinguish between males and females.

- Oviraptors share many characteristics with birds, and may have been covered in feathers.

## Wrongly accused

The original fossil find was misinterpreted by the scientists that studied it. They found the fossil of the Oviraptor near a nest containing dinosaur eggs – these eggs were assumed to belong to another dinosaur. The scientists thought the Ovirapor must have been stealing the eggs for food and so gave it its name of 'egg thief'.

In 1993 a team of American and Mongolian scientists found a fossil of an egg of the same kind – and this time found an Oviraptor embryo inside it. It seemed that the Oviraptor found in 1924 had been protecting its own nest!

Further evidence of the Oviraptor's 'nurturing' nature came with the discovery in 1995 of a fossil Oviraptor actually sitting on its nest. The Oviraptor had its feet folded underneath its body, and a clutch of at least 15 eggs were arranged in a circle and surrounded by its forearms.

## Reproduction

A recent discovery from Jiangxi in China showed a partial skeleton of an Oviraptor who was about to give birth, with intact eggs with shells still inside the body. Examination of the

find showed that the reproductive system of an Oviraptor is something between that of reptiles and birds, having similarities to each. This is taken as further evidence of the theory that birds evolved from dinosaurs.

## Dinosaur Data

| PRONUNCIATION: | O-VIH-**RAP**-TOR |
| SUBORDER: | THERAPODA |
| FAMILY: | OVIRAPTORIDAE |
| DESCRIPTION: | BIPEDAL OMNIVORE |
| FEATURES: | TOOTHLESS BEAK, HORNY CREST IN TOP OF HEAD |
| DIET: | OMNIVOROUS |

# ACROCANTHOSAURUS

## Gigantic bipedal hunter

Acrocanthosaurus means 'high-spined lizard'. It gets this name from the unusual spikes which grew out of its spine.

## Appearance

'Acro' (as the dinosaur is often nicknamed) was 13 m (42 ft) in length and weighed 2300 kg (5,000 lb). Acro's teeth were designed for tearing meat from the bones of its prey, not for crushing and cracking.

Acro was a meat eater, and had a skull very similar to that of Allosaurus. It had typical Allosaur 'eye horns', developed into ridges to protect the eyes –

a second ridge ran along the top of the nose and joined up with the eye ridges. The unusually deep back part of its lower jaw gave it a very powerful bite. Its hands were nothing like an Allosaur's, however – it had three-fingered hands equipped with sickle-shaped claws, shaped for holding prey rather than puncturing skin.

## The spines

The tall spines on the backbone of Acrocanthosaurus ran from its neck down to the front half of its tail.

### FOSSIL FACTS
**Fossils have been found in Oklahoma, Texas, Utah and Arizona, all in the USA. The first specimens were found in the early 1950s, and a complete skeleton was discovered in Atoka County (Oklahoma) in 1983 by Cephis Hall and Sid Love.**

| Permian period | Triassic period | Jurassic period | Cretaceous period |
|---|---|---|---|
| 290-248 million years ago) | (248-176 million years ago) | (176-130 million years ago) | (130-65 million years ago) |

Scientists originally thought this must mean it had a 'sail' on its back like Dimetrodon. More recent thinking is that had more of a 'hump-backed' shape than a sail, but the exact purpose of the spines is still a mystery.

They may have been anchors for powerful muscles. If so, it would mean Acro was very strong indeed – and it would have needed to be to catch the huge sauropod dinosaurs its fossilised footprints show it tracking! Some modern animals, for example, elephants, horses and buffalo, have this kind of muscle suspension.

The spines might also have been used to communicate with other Acros, and to regulate body temperature. They would have provided Acro with extra surface area, which would be helpful for both the display of colour and pattern, and for absorbing and getting rid of heat. This would have been very useful in the tropical climate in which it lived.

## Dinosaur Data

| | |
|---|---|
| PRONUNCIATION: | AK-ROW-**KAN**-THO-**SAWR**-US |
| SUBORDER: | THERAPODA |
| DESCRIPTION: | LARGE, POWERFUL MEAT EATER |
| FEATURES: | TALL RIDGE SPINES |
| DIET: | CARNIVORE AND POSSIBLY SCAVENGER |

# MEGA FACTS

- This dinosaur would probably be able to lift a small car off the ground if it were alive today. Its arms were larger and more powerful than those of T-Rex itself.

- Acrocanthosaurus appeared in the multi-platform video game *Jurassic Park: Operation Genesis.* It is shown catching a Dryosaurus for dinner.

- In 2005, scientists constructed a replica of Acro's brain, using CT scanning technology on a fossil skull. The result showed that the brain was more like that of a crocodile than a bird in shape, that Acro probably had excellent hearing, and that its head would have been held at an angle 25 degrees beneath horizontal.

- As any of its 68 serrated teeth broke, another was ready to take its place. Like a shark, Acro was constantly shedding old teeth and replacing them with new ones.

- In 1998, the fossil skeleton of an Acrocanthosaurus nicknamed 'Fran' was bought for the North Carolina Museum of Natural Sciences for $3 million, believed to be the second highest price ever paid for a dinosaur.

# ALLOSAURUS

## Dominant flesh eater

MEAT EATERS

### FOSSIL FACTS
**Fossils have been found in the Western USA and (recently) in Europe. The first fossils were found in Colarado, USA.**

very powerful arms. It also had large claws on its hands – one claw discovered was more than 350 cm (11 ft) long.

Allosaurus was light thanks to air sacs in its bones – this would have allowed it to run very fast, and also to leap at its prey, tear out a chunk with its teeth and then leap away again.

Allosaurus means 'different lizard', so named because its vertebrae (backbones) were different from those of all other dinosaurs. The first specimen was studied and named by Othniel C. March in 1877.

### Appearance

Allosaurus was between 7–12 m (23–39 ft) in length, 3–4.5 m (10–15 ft) tall and weighed 1,000–4,500 kg (1–4 tons). It had a huge head, long strong hind legs and

## Dinosaur Data

| | |
|---|---|
| PRONUNCIATION: | AL-UH-**SAWR**-US |
| SUBORDER: | THERAPODA |
| FAMILY: | ALLOSAURIDAE |
| DESCRIPTION: | BIPEDAL CARNIVORE |
| FEATURES: | HINGED JAW, BLUNT HORNS |
| DIET: | PLANT-EATING DINOSAURS |

| Permian period | Triassic period | Jurassic period | Cretaceous period |
|---|---|---|---|
| (290-248 million years ago) | (248-176 million years ago) | (176-130 million years ago) | (130-66 million years ago) |

Allosaurus was the most common large predator in North America 155–145 million years ago – so many fossil remains have been found in this area that some scientists suggest Allosaurus might have hunted in large packs.

## Skeletons

In 1991, a 95% complete skeleton of a young Allosaurus was discovered and named 'Big Al'. Big Al was 8 m (26 ft) in length and 19 of his bones showed signs of breakage or infection. He was discovered by a Swiss team led by Kirby Siber. The same team later excavated an even more impressive Allosaurus skeleton – the best preserved of its kind to date – which was promptly christened 'Big Al 2'.

## Attacking prey

Recently, more information has come to light about the way an Allosaurus attacked its prey. A scientist at Cambridge University (England) called Emily Rayfield created a computer model of Big Al's skull, using techniques usually used in engineering.

The model allowed her to calculate the force that Big Al's jaws would have needed to break the skull of a living creature. She concluded that Allosaurus actually had quite a weak bite.

The skull was also very light, but capable of withstanding massive upwards force. Rayfield concluded that the Allosaur had actually attacked by opening its mouth wide and using powerful neck muscles to drive its upper jaw downward, slamming into its prey like an axe and tearing away hunks of flesh.

# MEGA FACTS

- Allosaurus jaws were able to 'expand' to allow larger chunks of food to be swallowed.

- Allosaurus has featured in several films.

- Footprint evidence suggests that Allosaurus hunted in packs, and may have raised its young in large nests.

- An Allosaurus could run at almost 60 km/h (37 mph).

# SAURORNITHOIDES

## Big-brained bird-like carnivore

Saurornithoides means 'bird-like lizard'. It was named in 1924 by Osborn and comes from the Greek stems *saur* (lizard) *ornitho* (bird) and *oid* (form).

Like other members of its family, Saurornithoides was a highly-efficient predator. It had a long, low head and sharp, closely-packed teeth. Like other raptors, it ran on its strong hind legs and probably used its long arms and grasping hands to seize and tear at live prey, including small mammals and possibly other dinosaur hatchlings.

It had one especially long, vicious claw on its hind feet, which was attached to the fourth toe, and was retractable when running or walking.

Much of what we know about this dinosaur comes from fossilised skull material – no complete skeleton has been found anywhere.

### Dinosaur Data

| | |
|---|---|
| PRONUNCIATION: | **SAWR**-OR-NIH-**THOY**-DEEZ |
| SUBORDER: | THERAPODA |
| FAMILY: | TROODONTIDAE |
| DESCRIPTION: | BIRD-LIKE BIPEDAL CARNIVORE |
| FEATURES: | HUGE RETRACTABLE CLAW, BIG BRAIN |
| DIET: | SMALLER MAMMALS, INSECTS |

### FOSSIL FACTS
**Fossils have been found in Mongolia. The first fossil was found in the 1920s by an expedition led by Roy Chapman Andrews.**

## Skulls

The skull fossils show that
Saurornithoides had a very large
brain compared to the size of its body, making it one of the
most intelligent of the dinosaurs. Its brain was six times
as big as that of a crocodile.

The skulls also show that this dinosaur had
large eyes, positioned forward so as to
give it binocular vision. This would have
been a big help while hunting – for
example, allowing Saurornithoides to
accurately judge distances. Most
dinosaurs had eyes on the sides of
their heads. It probably also had
excellent night vision, and may even
have been primarily nocturnal.

When the first Saurornithoides fossils were discovered,
its long, narrow snout tricked those studying it into thinking it
was actually an ancient bird. There is still debate as to just
how like a bird the 'lizard bird form' really was. Many
scientists, for example, now believe its body may have been
covered in feathers. Further study (and, hopefully,
new discoveries) will be needed before
the secrets of this smart little
dinosaur are revealed.

# MEGA FACTS

- Estimated to be 2–3 m (6–10 ft) in length.

- Weighed about 13–27 kg (29–59 lb).

- Fossils from very similar dinosaurs have been found in North America, suggesting that 85–77 million years ago, the climates of Mongolia and North America were similar.

- It was a smart dinosaur as it had the biggest brain relative to its body size of any of the dinosaurs.

- It was also sharp-eyed as it had large eyes and binocular vision.

# CARNOTAURUS

## Horned gigantic carnivore

## FOSSIL FACTS
The first (and only) fossil of the Carnotaurus was found in Patagonia (South America) in 1985 by José F. Bonaparte.

Carnotaurus means 'meat-eating bull'. It was named in 1985 by José F. Bonaparte. It is named from its most notable feature – the two horns located above its eyes, resembling those of a bull. The name comes from the Greek words *carn* (flesh) and *taurus* (bull).

The purpose of these horns is not known. It is possible that they were used for display – for attracting mates, or showing dominance.

Carnotaurus grew to about 7.6 m (25 ft) long and stood about 4.6 m (15 ft) tall on its hind legs. It moved on two feet and had a long thin tail. We do not know if it had the speed and agility to hunt down prey, but its short, pointed teeth show us it was a meat eater. Instead of hunting, it may have scavenged from the bodies of dead animals.

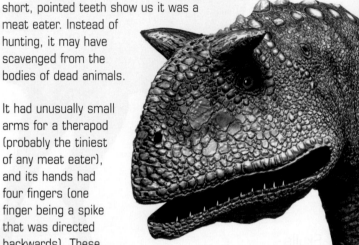

It had unusually small arms for a therapod (probably the tiniest of any meat eater), and its hands had four fingers (one finger being a spike that was directed backwards). These fingers had sharp claws, which it used to hold and tear at its food. The Carnotaurus' hands do not bend and, strangely, seem to be attached directly to its body.

## Skull

The skull of Carnotaurus measures only 22 cm (9 in.), showing it had a much shorter snout that other therapods. Its eyes were set facing slightly forwards, so unlike most dinosaurs it may have had partial binocular vision (the ability to focus on one object with both eyes, which is very useful for judging distance).

This enormous dinosaur lived about 113–91 million years ago in what is now Argentina. It had a small skull, a broad chest and a thin tail.

## Appearance

Everything we know about Carnotaurus comes from one find, an almost complete skeleton. The skeleton was so well-preserved, it even kept impressions of the Carnotaurus' rough, bumpy skin all down its right hand side.

| Permian period | Triassic period | Jurassic period | Cretaceous period |
|---|---|---|---|
| 290-248 million years ago) | (248-176 million years ago) | (176-130 million years ago) | (130-66 million years ago) |

*Carnotaurus skeleton*

# MEGA FACTS

- A piece of fossilised skin from the head of a Carnotaurus shows a pattern of small scales, with larger scales covering prominent positions like the snout. These larger scales may have made these areas more colourful, as is quite common in lizards.

- More than five times as big as an African lion.

- Carnotaurus was one of the major villains in Disney's animated film *Dinosaur*.

- Carnotaurus weighed about 1,000 kg (1 ton).

- Carnotaurus featured in the Michael Crichton novel *The lost world*, but didn't make it into the film version – the film-makers opted for a Ceratosaurus instead.

## Dinosaur Data

| | |
|---|---|
| PRONUNCIATION: | **KAR**-NO-**TAWR**-US |
| SUBORDER: | THERAPODA |
| FAMILY: | ABELISAURIDAE |
| DESCRIPTION: | HORNED CARNIVORE |
| FEATURES: | EYEHORNS, TINY ARMS |
| DIET: | OTHER DINOSAURS, MAY HAVE SCAVENGED ON DEAD BODIES |

27

# TROODON

## Intelligent bipedal dinosaur

### Appearance

Troodon was a biped with long hind legs, relatively short arms, a long thin jaw with sharp serrated teeth and a stiff tail that would have helped it balance when running and leaping.

It weighed about 60 kg (175 lb). It was about 3.5 m (12 ft) long and 1 m (3 ft) tall at the hips.

Its long hind legs had large, sickle-shaped claws on the second toes of each foot. Troodon used these claws for kicking into its prey, to cause terrible wounds and prevent it being thrown off as it used its teeth and front claws to bite and tear. The sickle claws were much longer than the other toes' claws and would have been kept

Troodon was discovered by Ferdinand Hayden in 1855 and named by Joseph Leidy in 1856. The name means 'wounding tooth'. It was named after the serrated tooth that was the first fragment of its skeleton to be found.

*Troodon tooth*

## Dinosaur Data

| | |
|---|---|
| PRONUNCIATION: | **TRUE**-OH-DON |
| SUBORDER: | THEROPODA |
| FAMILY: | TROODONTIDAE |
| DESCRIPTION: | LARGE-EYED INTELLIGENT DINOSAUR |
| FEATURES: | LARGE BRAIN, PARTIALLY OPPOSABLE THUMBS, SICKLE-SHAPED TOE CLAW, LARGE EYES |
| DIET: | LIZARDS, SNAKES, SMALL MAMMALS AND OTHER SMALL CREATURES |

| Permian period | Triassic period | Jurassic period | Cretaceous period |
|---|---|---|---|
| (290-248 million years ago) | (248-176 million years ago) | (176-130 million years ago) | (130-66 million years ago) |

pointing upwards when running or walking. Its arms had a bird-like wrist joint that allowed them to fold in and back, rather like a bird folds its wings.

## Hunting

Troodon had large eyes that would have enabled it to see well in the dark. They were also slightly forward facing which have allowed it limited binocular vision.

Troodon had a large brain to body size ratio, strongly suggesting it was one of the most intelligent dinosaurs.

Troodon had partially opposable thumbs, which would have helped it grasp branches and other objects more firmly. The opposable thumb was vital in human evolution as it allowed us to manipulate tools.

Troodon probably hunted at dusk or twilight when its night vision would give it an advantage. Troodon would have hunted small mammals and lizards and perhaps baby dinosaurs.

# MEGA FACTS

- One of the first dinosaurs found in North America.

- Troodon may have supplemented its diet with plants, making it an omnivore.

- Fossilised Troodon nests have been found, suggesting that Troodon brooded over its eggs rather like hens.

- Had they not become extinct, dinosaurs like Troodon with their opposable thumbs and large brains might have developed to become intelligent creatures. In the 1980s, palaeontologist Dale Russell worked with artist Ron Sequin to produce a model of an upright dinosaur called Dinosauroid to show what such a creature could have looked like.

- Troody is a robotic Troodon built at MIT, to simulate how these creatures walked.

**Troody**
(1996, 2001)
(Courtesy of Peter Dilworth)

Troody was developed at the MIT Artificial Intelligence Lab. Its design is based on the carnivorous dinosaur Troodon formosus. Troody could stand up from a rest position and then walk. Troody could even sense when it was walking on an uneven surface and adjust its steps to the terrain.

# MEGALOSAURUS

## Huge bipedal

### FOSSIL FACTS
**Fossils have been found in Europe, Asia, Africa and South America.**

This carnivore grew to a length of 9 m (30 ft), a height of 3.7 m (12 ft). It was bipedal. It had a long tail to help balance out its heavy head.

Its back legs were much longer than its arms. The arms had hands that could have been used for grasping. The legs ended in four-toed feet (one toe was reversed, like all therapod dinosaurs). Both fingers and toes had strong, sharp claws.

### Diet

Megalosaurus was a powerful hunter, and could attack even the largest prey. It would have hunted plant-eating

Megalosaurus means 'great lizard'. It was named in 1824 and was the first dinosaur to be given a scientific name.

### Appearance

No complete skeleton has yet been discovered so we cannot be 100% certain of what it looked like.

Megalosaurus had a big head, and its curved teeth had saw edges well suited to eating meat. Its jaws were very powerful. It had small eyes with bony knobs over the top of them and its head was held up by a strong, short neck.

### Dinosaur Data

| | |
|---|---|
| PRONUNCIATION: | **MEG**-UH-LOW-**SAWR**-US |
| SUBORDER: | THERAPODA |
| FAMILY: | MEGALOSAURIDAE |
| DESCRIPTION: | LARGE BIPEDAL CARNIVORE |
| FEATURES: | POWERFUL JAWS, BULKY BODY, LARGE HEAD |
| DIET: | OTHER DINOSAURS |